THE LOVE THAT NEVER LEFT

BETWEEN GOODBYE AND FOREVER

ANU SINGH

Made with ♥ on the Notion Press Platform
www.notionpress.com

Thank You

To my husband,

You have given me the space to dream,

the courage to write, and the strength to be myself.

With your quiet support, I have found the freedom to pour my
heart onto these pages.

Thank you for believing in me always,

With your belief, even the wind carries my dreams—

and for that, my heart bows in gratitude.

Thank you, My Dearest Friends

This book holds pieces of my soul, but you—

you have held me.

Through quiet nights and stormy days,

through laughter that echoed and silences that spoke louder
than words,

you have been my safe place.

This book is mine, but the strength behind it is yours.

For every word I wrote, for every truth I dared to speak,

for simply being there—thank you.

Acknowledgements

Some people come into our lives not to stay, but to teach us something profound. Their presence feels like destiny, their love like poetry written in the stars. And yet, life has its own way of unfolding—sometimes, the ones we hold closest are the ones we must learn to live without.

This book is not just a story of two souls; it is a story of love that transcends time, a connection that remains even in silence. It is for those who have loved deeply but could not be together, for those who have moved forward yet still carry an unspoken void within them. You do not need them in your life anymore, yet their absence shapes you, lingers in quiet moments, and exists in the spaces between words left unsaid.

Perhaps, in ways we cannot always understand, their absence is what was meant for us. Perhaps, love does not need presence to be eternal.

Every word in this book has been written from the depths of my heart, hoping to capture the emotions of those who have ever loved, lost, and yet never truly let go. May you find a part of your own story in these verses, and may they remind you that love, in all its forms, is never incomplete—it simply transforms.

This book is not an ending; it is proof that love, once felt, never truly leaves.

The Love That Never Left

Be Soft, Be Love
Love yourself the way the earth holds the rain—
without questioning if it is enough, without asking when it
will return.
You do not need to be whole for someone to love you,
but you must allow yourself to be seen.

Give space, not as a distance but as an offering.
Love is not meant to be held too tightly;
it needs room to breathe, to move, to choose.

Be soft, even when the world is not.
Let love come and go as it must.
Let it teach you, let it shape you,
but never let it make you afraid of opening your heart again.

Love cannot be forced
nor earned by sacrifice.
It is not a barter,
but a divine exchange of souls,
dancing in harmony.
If you are giving all you have,
and the other receives little,
Pause.
Do not empty yourself,
for you are not meant to be drained.
Love is not a transaction,
it is a flow—
a current that rises and falls,
but always returns.
You deserve a love that mirrors your own,
love that lifts you,
not one that asks you to surrender your peace.
Let go of what does not return your flame,
and make space for the love that chooses you—
freely, completely.

There are souls you meet, and without reason or explanation,
you recognize them—not with your eyes, but with something deeper.
A knowing that stretches beyond this life, beyond names,
as if the universe whispered your existence into the same breath.

They come as lovers, as friends, as kindred spirits,
or as something nameless yet undeniable.
No effort, no questioning—just an unspoken harmony,
like the sea knowing the shore, like the moon finding the tide.

They arrive out of nowhere, in the strangest of ways,
yet they awaken something dormant within you.
A flicker of belonging, a glimpse of eternity,
a feeling that reminds you—you are alive.

Does this make me believe in fate, in destiny, in the unseen hand of the Divine?
Perhaps. Perhaps not.
But it makes me believe in something greater than chance.
Something that moves unseen, weaving lives together
in ways we may never understand yet always feel.

Some loves are not meant to arrive,
only to hover like the scent of rain—
near, yet never falling.

What of the one who walks beside you
but never crosses the threshold of your world?
What of the love that blooms in silence,
that lingers like a half-whispered prayer,
waiting, always waiting?

It is easy to mourn what is lost,
but how do you grieve what was never yours?
How do you silence a love
that still breathes in the hollow spaces of your soul,
that still waits at the door,
though it was never invited in?

Not everyone is meant to stay,
not every love is meant to belong—
but some of us carry it anyway,
some of us must.

It aches, doesn't it?
To weave your soul into words,
to send them into the void,
only to be met with silence.

You whisper to the wind,
"Am I not worth her first step?
Does she not carry this longing as I do?"

But love does not always wear its name out loud.
Sometimes, silence is not absence—
but a battle unseen,
a fear unspoken,
a storm she fights alone.

And yet, your heart waits.
It listens for the softest echo,
the faintest spark—
a sign she remembers,
that she aches as you do.

And in this waiting,
your love stretches,
fragile as a thread of light,

yet unbroken,
yet infinite.

My heart overflows with a love so vast,
that it aches to pour itself into her soul.
I wish to cradle her joy in my hands,
to see her smile brighter than the sun.

I want to hold her close,
not for a moment, but for eternity—
not bound by time, nor by space.
Even if life separates our paths,
my love will find her in the quiet hours,
whispering through the wind,
resting in the warmth of her dreams.

To love her is not a choice,
it is the essence of my being.
Together or apart,
she will always be the one
I carry within me,
the one my love will forever call home.

You came into my life like a quiet storm,
filling spaces
I didn't know were empty.
I told myself I wouldn't love you,
but how does one deny the ocean
when it calls your soul to drown?

You weren't just someone I cared for—
you became the air I breathed,
the thought I carried,
the place I belonged.

Every moment with you felt like a paradise,
and every moment without you feels like an ache
that sits quietly in my chest,
unseen but always there.

With you, I saw the world's colors anew,
felt the warmth of the sun
that I didn't know had risen within me.

And even if I move forward,
it is not without carrying
this endless love
that no time or distance can diminish.
You are my beginning,
my forever,

and the part of me
I will never let go.

Our love is always enough,
not because it fills the cracks of the world,
but because it exists,
breathing quietly between us,
like the wind that moves without needing to be seen.

It does not demand more than it gives,
nor does it falter in the face of absence.
It is the silent knowing,
the unbroken thread that binds two souls
beyond time, beyond space.

Even when the storms come,
when the earth trembles beneath us,
our love remains,
like a tree rooted deep,
its strength unseen but unshaken.

It does not ask for perfection,
it does not seek to be proven.
Our love is,
and that is always enough.

She says I do not feel her absence,
that her leaving was nothing but a passing breeze to me.
But how do I tell her, beloved,
that the wind still carries her name,
that the earth beneath my feet remembers her steps?

Since she left, the sun has risen a thousand times,
but not once has it warmed me.
I walk, I breathe, I exist—
but I have not lived.

Perhaps she has left our story in the past,
but I remain where she last held me,
a traveler who never moved,
a heart that still beats in the rhythm of her farewell.

And look—
today, I am writing a book
woven with the echoes of her laughter,
stitched with the memories she left behind.
She may never read these words,
but they will always belong to her.

I will never forget you,
nor do I wish to.

Why should I erase the moments
that painted my soul with light?

Why should I silence the echoes
of a love that still breathes within me?

Every moment with you
was a jewel placed gently in my hands—
a treasure I refuse to lose.

Time may pull us apart,
but I will carry you,
not as a wound,
but as the most beautiful verse
written upon my heart.

The love I give her feels endless,
a river that never ceases to flow.
But her love—oh, her love—
it is the ocean that holds my river,
vast, boundless, and deeper than I can fathom.

She loves me in ways
words cannot reach,
in silences that speak louder
than all the world's songs.

Her love cradles my soul,
gentler than the softest breeze,
yet stronger than the pull of the earth.

What I give, she returns tenfold,
a love so abundant
it leaves me in awe,
grateful to exist in its embrace.

I need her,
like the parched earth waits for rain,
like a lone nightingale sings to the moon,
aching for the touch of dawn.

I do not wish to hold her with hands alone,
but with the weight of longing in my soul.
There is a storm within me,
and only her embrace can quiet the thunder.

How many words have drowned in my silence?
How many prayers have whispered her name?
I long to pour them into her,
to let my heart speak where my lips could not.

I ask for nothing but her time, her nearness.
Not the sun, not the stars—only her.
For to be beside her,
is to stand in the doorway of home,
where my heart has always belonged.

I had seen her before—
a fleeting presence, a name without a story,
a passing moment in the rhythm of ordinary days.
But that day, something shifted,
as if the air around us had been waiting
for this very moment to unfold.

She spoke, and the quiet between us
became laughter—carefree, boundless,
like the wind dancing with untold secrets.
She was light, unburdened,
a soul that refused to be contained.

And in that quiet, unspoken moment,
something within me whispered—
she will matter.

I saw a soul unlike any other.
She moved through life as the wind moves through open
fields—
free, fearless, unbound.

Nothing could contain her,
no walls, no rules, no weight of the world.
She lived as if life itself was a song
meant to be danced to, not obeyed.

Yet, beneath that wild spirit,
there was a kindness so rare,
a gentleness she gave only to me.

She cared without asking,
watched over me without chains,
and in her presence,
I felt both held and set free.

It began as something gentle,
something unspoken yet deeply felt.
Her presence held a warmth
I had been searching for it all my life.
With her, time did not move—
or perhaps it moved too fast,
slipping through my fingers
like grains of golden sand.
Morning would fade into evening,
yet I never wished to leave.
She was not just comfort—
she was peace, a quiet belonging,
a place where my soul could rest.

Whenever it was time to leave,
her fingers were reluctant to let go of mine.
At first, it was just a touch—
a fleeting moment, a silent wish.
But soon, our hugs grew longer as if time itself had slowed,
whispering, *Stay a little more.*
That moment of parting felt unbearable,
as if the air between us stretched too thin,
as if the distance was a cruel trick the world played on us.
We would return to our homes, but our hearts never left.
The night became ours again—
through whispered calls and unread messages,
we found ways to close the space that life had placed
between us.

I do not know when it began—
this silent pull toward her world,
this forgetting of time in her presence.

She spoke, and laughter poured from her lips
like a river that had never known drought.
Her words were light as air,
yet they settled deep within me.

I told myself— *just a little longer,*
but time bowed to her,
folded itself beneath her smile,
and let me stay.

Was it her home that called me back,
or was it the way she made the air feel softer,
the hours feel lighter,
as if I had stepped into a place
where the heart no longer carried weight?

I stayed.
And the sun dipped,
and the stars arrived,
and still, I stayed.

We drifted toward each other,
like rivers drawn to the same sea,
merging without question,
without fear.

In her presence,
the noise of the world fell away,
and silence became a sacred song,
a prayer I had unknowingly sought.

Resting in her lap
was resting in the arms of the Divine—
as if the heavens whispered,
"Here, there is nothing more to seek."

When she held me,
it was not mere touch,
but a binding of souls,
a silent prayer to time itself:
"Do not move; do not take this away."

Her embrace grew deeper,
like roots refusing to let go of the earth,
and in that moment,

without words, we told the universe—
"Separation is an illusion."

In her eyes,
I did not find a stranger—
I found the echo of my soul,
a piece of myself I had long abandoned.

She did not heal me with promises
nor with grand gestures of love.
She simply was—
and in her being, I became whole.

She never sought to bind me,
never wished to keep me caged.
Yet, in her presence,
I felt freer than the sky,
lighter than a drifting cloud.

She gave me nothing to hold,
yet I walked away with everything.
For in her, I found not just love—
but the courage to love myself.

With her, I was unchained,
as if the wind itself had whispered—
"Be free."

I had never met someone like her before,
fearless, untamed,
laughing in the face of rules
as if life was hers to command.

She carried no weight of the world,
and in her presence,
neither did I.

The quiet girl I had always been
vanished like mist in the sun.
With her, I was light, wild, alive.

She made me feel—
not just safe, but seen.
Not just accepted but understood.
And for the first time,
I was not just living,
I was *being.*

I could not name this feeling,
nor shape it into words.
It was new, strange, yet deeply familiar—
like a forgotten melody returning to my soul.

Something was shifting,
a quiet pull toward her,
a warmth I had never known before.
Was it love? Was it something more?
I did not know, and yet,
I did not want to escape it.

She and I—
we laughed, we wandered,
we lived as if the world did not exist,
as if time had no claim over us.

What was this bond,
so effortless, so free?
Perhaps some feelings are not meant to be understood—
only felt,
only lived,
only surrendered to.

We lived in a world of quiet joy,
where mornings began with melodies,
and love spoke not through words,
but through the language of glances.

She sang, and the air grew softer,
her voice a river that carried me
to a place where only we existed.

We counted the day in embraces,
arms wrapped around each other
as if the world would vanish
if we let go too soon.

We ate side by side,
shared laughter between bites,
and when the world grew too loud,
I found my refuge—
my head resting in her lap,
her fingers weaving stories in my hair.

She spoke of small, silly things,
her words like petals falling into silence,
and I laughed,
not at what she said,
but at the way she filled the spaces
I never knew they were empty.

Oh, what peace it was to be near her,
To be held in the quiet strength of her care.

The days of togetherness were slipping,
like sand through open fingers.
We knew—
one day, too soon,
we would no longer wake to the same sun,
no longer share the same quiet spaces.

Yet we never spoke of endings.
Why chase sorrow before it arrives?
Why cloud the present
with shadows of the inevitable?

I told myself—
when the moment comes,
we will part, as all things do.
But now, we are here.
Now, the air still carries her laughter,
her warmth still lingers beside me.

So I did not count the days.
I did not measure time.
I only lived,
fully, fiercely,
as if love itself could hold back the dawn
just a little longer.

And then, the day arrived—
the one we always knew would come.
No matter how right it felt,
no matter how deeply we belonged,
we were never meant to stay.

From the very beginning,
fate had written a different ending,
and now, it stood before us,
waiting to be spoken aloud.

So I said the words—
soft, breaking, final.
"We cannot talk anymore."

She did not argue,
did not hold on.
She simply accepted
what we had always known.

And just like that,
the silence between us
became permanent.

And from that day forward,

we walked away—

not because we wanted to,

but because we had to.

The road was cruel,

scattered with the weight of unsaid words,

but we did not turn back.

We learned to live in silence,

to bear the distance like an old wound

that never truly heals.

Neither of us reached out,

and neither of us broke the vow.

But in the quiet, I found my refuge—

I wrote.

Poems, whispers, prayers—

all in her name, all for her memory.

Not to bring her back,

not to reopen wounds,

but to keep the love unbroken,

to let it live where it no longer hurts.

And so it began—
this endless ritual of remembering.
She lived in every moment,
in every breath I took,
a presence unseen but never absent.

Time passed, but nothing changed.
Even now, she lingers,
a shadow in my quietest thoughts.
I miss her, not with longing,
but with a softness, a knowing—
that she was, that she mattered.

But I do not wish for her return.
Not anymore.
When we parted, life moved swiftly.
My world changed, vows were made,
and she, with all her love,
chose to step away—
not for lack of feeling,
but so I could live in peace.

She was never a storm to break me,
only the wind that knew
When to let go.

I sometimes sent words like birds into the sky,
hoping they would land in her heart.
She listened but never spoke,
her silence stretching between us
like an ocean, I could not cross.

I knocked at the door of her soul,
but she stood behind it, unmoved.
Had she forgotten the language of my longing,
or was she too weary to answer?

I filled with questions,
why had she turned to stone?
Had I loved alone,
or had she buried her love in a place
where even she could not find it?

She had become a quiet river,
flowing away without a sound.
But tell me, beloved—
is silence truly emptiness,
or does it hold more sorrow
than words can bear?

I know she walks through storms unseen,
carrying burdens the world does not know.
Her silence is not a wound,
but the echo of battles only she can fight.

How can I grieve her distance,
when love is not a chain,
but a river—
flowing where it must,
holding both sorrow and grace?

I ask for nothing,
but that peace may find her,
that the weight she carries
may become light as a feather in the wind.

Even from afar, my heart remains,
not as a longing, not as a demand,
but as a quiet prayer—
a flame that flickers in the dark,
a whisper of warmth in the cold.

Years later, when our paths cross again,

there will be no need for time's inventions.

No clocks, no machines—

just the way your eyes find mine,

and in that single glance, the years will vanish.

Time will fold itself like a story unfinished,

and the past will breathe once more.

Every echo of laughter, every whispered word,

every touch that ever lingered

will rise between us, untouched by distance.

No words will be needed,

for silence will hold more weight than speech.

And in your gaze, I will see it all—

not just the past, not just the years lost,

but the eternity that was always ours.

I never told you,
"I love you,"
because love was already breathing between us,
in the spaces, words could never fill.

Your hand in mine,
a language only our souls understood.
Your laughter
was a melody that softened my heart.

We did not speak of love,
we lived it—
in the way your eyes held mine,
in that way, the silence felt whole with you.

Why say the river flows
when its song is everywhere?
Why name the sun's warmth
when it wraps you in its quiet light?
With you,
"I love you" was never spoken,
because we were love,
without needing to be told.

You made me a writer,
but not with ink or quill,
you carved words into my soul
with the quiet ache of your absence.

Whenever I miss you,
the skies open inside me,
and I write to pour out the storm,
to hold you in lines and whispers
where my hands cannot reach.

I write all day,
each letter a thread to weave you closer,
each word a prayer to the moments
when your presence filled the air.

You are the muse I never sought,
but the one my heart found in its longing.
Your name spills onto every page,
not in sound, but in essence,
a silent hymn to the love
that lives between what was and what is.

So I write, not to forget you,
but to keep you breathing in my world.
For you are the ink,
and I am merely the page

you left your heart upon.

There was a time—
a handful of stolen days—
when life was kind,
when the universe whispered our names
like a prayer meant to last forever.

But time is a fickle guest,
never staying, never waiting.
It gave us moments,
then vanished,
leaving me to wander a world
where you are no longer mine.

Why could my existence
not begin and end in your arms?
Why was I left
to learn the art of breathing without you,
of walking roads where your footsteps do not echo?

If only life had folded itself
when those days ended,
I would never have known
the ache of an unfinished story.

I miss her like the night misses the moon,
aching for her light in the endless dark.
I wish to send my words to her,
but fear whispers—
what if her silence is all I find?

Does she long for me as I do for her?
Does my name ever stir in her heart?
If she misses me,
why does the wind not carry her voice to me?

I wait, like a desert for rain,
for her to break this stillness,
to tell me she loves me,
to tell me she remembers.

Her silence rests heavy in my soul,
yet even in this quiet pain,
I hold her—
for her absence is still my connection to her.

Sometimes I wonder,
Did she took my love for granted?
Does the weight of my longing
go unnoticed, unanswered?
No matter how many messages I send,
her silence lingers like a closed door.

And then, a quiet doubt blooms—
does she truly deserve this love,
this endless offering of my heart?
For her side feels like a distant shore,
untouched by the tides I send.

But love, true love,
is not a balance to measure.
It is a fire that burns,
even when it warms only one.

Yet, I ache.
Not for her response,
but for the knowing
that I have given my all,
and she has yet to see
the temple I built in her name.

When I first met her,
I could not have known
that her soul would one day
become the axis of my world.

I did not see the storm she carried,
the quiet love waiting to bloom.
I did not feel the weight of her absence
that now lingers in every breath.

The time we shared—
those simple, fleeting moments—
have carved themselves into my heart,
etched deeper than I ever imagined.

How could I have known
that she would become so vital,
like air to my lungs,
like light to my weary soul?

In her, I found a home,
but I never realized
how much I'd miss the warmth
until it was gone.

A year passed in unspoken longing—
no calls, no letters,
only the weight of absence
settling between us like an untold story.

Yet in that silence, I still wrote to her,
sent whispers into the void,
knowing they would never reach her hands.

Then sorrow found me,
a darkness so deep
it felt as if the earth itself was slipping away.

But love does not need words to hear—
she knew.
And in that knowing,
the silence shattered.

Message after message,
her love broke through the distance,
a flood of tenderness
rushing to hold me before I fell too far.

She wept, she prayed,
her heart reaching for me
as if sheer longing
could keep my breath steady.

Perhaps it did.

For a moment,
we became whole again,
wrapped in a love
that time could not erase.

But love is not always a door—
sometimes, it is only a window,
showing us what we cannot hold.

And so, we stepped away once more—
not because the love had faded,
but because the world
was never kind enough to let us stay.

She told me— "I love you, not to keep, but to let you bloom.
I miss you, not to pull you back, but to watch you soar."

I must always be okay, she said.
No matter where life takes me,
no matter who stands beside me.
She only wants my joy,
even if it is joy without her.

She will learn to live without me,
if my world is whole,
if my heart is unbroken.
She needs nothing from me,
and yet, she will always love me.

What is love, if not the art of giving?
What is devotion, if not the courage to say—
"Go, if you must. But know, I will love you still."

She loves me—
not in the way the world understands,
not with hands that cling,
but with a heart that prays in silence.

She has whispered it a thousand times,
not in words,
but in the way she watches me,
in the way, she folds her longing into quiet blessings.

And yet, she stepped away—
not because her love wavered,
but because it burned too fiercely
to keep me bound.

She wanted me to be the sky,
even if it meant she could only be the wind—
always around me, yet never held.

Her love is not weak;
it is the ocean surrendering to the shore,
the moon offering its light to the night,
knowing it will never touch the sun.

She weeps where no one can see,
hides her trembling hands behind the walls of her silence.

She lets go, not because she does not love,
but because she loves me too much to ask me to stay.

Oh, how strange this love is—
a candle burning in an empty room,
a presence that lingers long after the footsteps fade.

She stands at a distance, unseen,
but her love is here,
woven into the air I breathe,
watching, waiting,
loving me in a way only the purest hearts can—
without wanting, without taking,
only giving, only blessing.

She asked me to move on,
to stop lingering in the echoes of what was.
She said my life should not begin and end with her,
that I must find my path,
a road untouched by her footsteps.

Her voice turned distant,
her words became walls,
each syllable pushing me further away.
She no longer wished to speak,
no longer wanted to hear
the longing in my silence.

But how does one walk away
when the heart stands still?
How does one unwrite a story
that was never meant to end?

She closed the door,
yet I stood outside,
unable to turn, unable to leave,
still carrying the love
she no longer wished to hold.

If she cares,
why does she turn away
when my heart reaches for her?

Why does she let me stand alone
beneath a sky heavy with storms,
as if my longing is too much to bear?

I unravel before her,
spill my ache at her feet,
but she walks away,
leaving only silence where her touch should be.

Her words arrive like whispered confessions,
gentle yet laced with thorns.

She speaks in echoes,
near yet distant,
always slipping through my hands
before I can hold her still.

How can a presence feel like home,
yet wound like a blade?

How can she pull me close,
only to let go
as if I was never meant to stay?

I do not understand the tides of her heart,
how she moves between light and shadow,
how she lingers yet never remains.

And yet—
even in her distance,
even in the ache she leaves behind,
I find myself waiting for her still.

We fight, and she looked away,

her silence swallowing my words.

I reach for her—

again, again—

but she is fire,

burning too bright to hold.

Each time,

I lose the battle before it begins.

Her anger stands tall,

unshaken, relentless,

while I kneel,

offering my surrender like a prayer.

I am tired of these storms,

of bending beneath their weight.

But still, I stay,

still, I reach,

as if the thunder will one day soften,

as if she will finally let the rain fall.

She wins every time,

but I am not sure what I lose anymore.

Pride?

Myself?

Or just the illusion

that she will ever turn back?

It hurt me deeply when she left
But when I reached for her,
she said she was hurt too—
that my leaving had broken something in her.
"This is your karma," she said.

And perhaps it was.
Perhaps love, too, has a way of balancing its scales.
I had wounded her once,
and now it was my turn to ache
in the silence, she left behind.

Guilt settled like a shadow in my chest,
until I looked back and saw—
I had chosen what was necessary,
not what was easy.
I had saved what could be saved,
knowing we were never meant
to stand in the same light forever.
So, I took my pain as an offering,
let it pass through me,
and let go of the guilt that held me captive.
For I had never wished to hurt her—
only to love her in the way fate had allowed.

I no longer called her, no longer sent messages.
Not that it mattered—
she had closed every door,
locked every way back to her world.
But I missed her.
Every day, every night,
in the spaces between thoughts,
she was there—
a whisper, a shadow,
a wound that refused to fade.
I asked the heavens,
"Why did she come into my life
only to leave me in ruins?"
Why did love, so deep, so rare,
become a sorrow I could not hold?
so I could finally let her go.

Why would the divine bring her into my life,
only to keep her just out of reach?

Why did her love, soft as a whisper,
find me, fill me,
only to leave an emptiness even deeper?

What kind of fate binds two souls so tightly,
only to unravel them,
setting them adrift like stars
too far apart to ever touch?

She is the light that once made me whole,
the echo in every quiet moment.
Yet our love remains unfinished—
a story with no final page,
only longing, only waiting.

Maybe some loves aren't meant to stay.
Maybe they exist to remind us
of something bigger than this world.

A love that never fades, never ends,
but lingers—
a fire burning across lifetimes.

When I was with you,
the world vanishes.
No noise, no time—
just the quiet hum of your presence
pulling me closer.

Your eyes become my horizon,
your touch, my anchor.

Everything else fades,
as if the universe exists
only in the space between us.

The stars could fall,
the sky could shatter,
but I would not look away.

For in your arms,
I have already found eternity.

Your breath is the whisper of the wind,
soft against my skin.

Your voice lingers in the air,
a melody I never want to end.

Every second with you feels stolen from time,

as if the universe itself pauses
just to watch us exist.
I do not ask for forever,
only for this moment—
to hold you,
to lose myself in you,
to love you
without the weight of the world.

Each morning,
you rise with the sun in my thoughts,
the first breath of my waking soul.

You linger through the hours,
a quiet presence in the
spaces between moments,
a melody only my heart can hear.

At night, I lay my head down,
and you slip into my dreams,
where time does not pull us apart,
where distance holds no power.

Even in silence, you are here—
woven into the rhythm of my days,
the echo in my solitude,
the unseen touch that lingers
long after you've gone.

How could I forget you
when you have become the pulse in my veins,
the unspoken prayer on my lips,
the presence I carry
through every rise and fall of time?

I think of those days,
when the sun rose,
and you were my morning,
your laughter my first light.

From dawn till dusk,
we shared a world of smiles,
your funny, cute expressions—
the ones you made when you pouted,
when you pretended to be mad.
How could something so simple
be so beautiful?

I remember the warmth of your hugs,
the hours we melted into each other,
as if the world outside ceased to exist.

We shared meals,
but it was more than food—
it was the way you looked at me,
the way you cared.
Even in silence,
you were my home.

You held my chaos gently,
shielding me with your kindness.
Now, these memories linger like a melody,

each note is a reminder
of those days we were us.

Missing you is the air I breathe,
a quiet rhythm that
hums beneath my days.

It is no longer a storm,
just a slow, steady rain,
soaking into every corner of me.

You are the sun I no longer see,
yet somehow, your warmth lingers.

Each day without you
has woven itself into me,
thread by thread,
until I no longer know where you end
and I begin.

Missing you is no longer a wound;
it is a habit,
an unspoken prayer,
a song I hum under my breath
just to keep you close.

I do not cry anymore.
The tears have turned to whispers,
whispers into silence.

But even in the silence,

you echo—

again and again,

a melody I will never stop hearing.

She calls me precious,
a word spoken with the softness
of a thousand prayers.

In the quiet moments of her day,
she holds my name in her heart,
sending it to the heavens
with each thought,
with every prayer,
a silent offering of love.

She reminds me,
in her gentle way,
to take care of myself,
to protect the spark within me,
for I am precious to her.

But her love is not
just spoken in words—
it is felt in the spaces between us,
in the stillness where
her thoughts linger,
always caring,
always protecting,
without ever asking for anything in return.

She loves me with depth

that mirrors the vastness of the oceans,

and in return,

I love her, not just for what she gives,

but for what she is—

a keeper of my heart,

a protector of my spirit,

the one who calls me precious,

and makes me believe it too.

I thought you were a passing breeze,
a gentle warmth, a fleeting light.

A presence soft as morning mist,
but not love—never love, not in my sight.

You held me like the quiet sky,
patient, vast, and full of grace.

Yet I wandered, blind and restless,
never knowing I had found my place.

And when we parted, I whispered lies—
Perhaps it was only the wind that touched me.

But time, the silent keeper of truth,
revealed the love I could not see.

Years have passed, faces fade,
but never has my soul known again
the way it ached when you were near,
the way it spoke your name like prayer.

Now I see, you were not a season,
not a wave that comes and goes.

You were the river I was meant to follow,

the sun behind my endless haze.

You were there, and I was blind.

Now you are gone, yet you remain—
not as memory, not as pain,
but as the love I never learned to name.

I love her in ways the world cannot hold,
like the wind loves the open sky,
like the river knows the sea
long before it arrives.

She is the fire that burns unseen,
a whisper in the heart of silence.
I call for nothing in return,
for love, once true,
asks only to be.

No hands have shaped this longing,
no time can measure its depth.

She walks through my soul
like a forgotten prayer
still echoing in the heavens.

She is not mine, nor am I hers,
yet in the spaces between our breaths,
we meet where the world dissolves,
where names are nothing
and only love remains.

The heart knows no past, no future,
only the endless moment of her.

I close my eyes, and she is there—
not as flesh, not as form,
but as the pulse of something eternal.

O love, nameless and boundless,
you are my night and my dawn,
the silence in which I am found,
the truth beyond the telling of it.

Though miles stretch between us,
you remain—
not in the space beside me,
but in the chambers of my soul,
where love neither fades nor forgets.

I search for you in the morning light,
in the hush of the stars,
in the quiet moments where longing blooms.
Your laughter lingers in the air,
your warmth still cradles my being.

What is the distance to love?
A mere illusion, a shadow passing.
For you are here, always,
woven into the breath of my existence.

Even in your absence, you are present.
Even in longing, you are home.
My love does not diminish—it deepens,
like a river meeting the sea,
like the sky surrendering to the sun.

And so I love you, not with hands that reach,
but with a heart that knows—
you were never far,
you were always within.

Kissing you—
on your lips,
on your cheeks,
on your forehead—
was like speaking a language
only we understood.

Hugging you all day,
feeling your heartbeat against mine,
was time itself standing still,
as if the world bowed
to our quiet union.

We laughed at silly things,
turned ordinary moments
into treasures.
Your hand in mine,
a soft, unspoken promise
that neither of us
would let go.

Every second with you
was a tapestry of beauty,
woven with love,

light,
and endless belonging.

She loved the scent of my being,
not the perfume, but something deeper—
the unspoken fragrance of my soul.

She would hold my shirt close,
breathe in the essence I left behind,
as if it whispered secrets only she could hear.

And I thought,
I will wear this perfume forever,
cling to it as if it could keep me near her,
as if its trace could tether her to me.

But I know,
what she loved was not bound by bottles or names—
it was the quiet song of our bond,
a scent that lingers
not on the skin,
but in the spaces between us.

Even if she passes me one day,
I hope the air will carry my memory to her,
and she will know me,
not by sight, but by the echo of what we once were.

I want all of you,
not in fleeting moments or borrowed days,
but in the infinite stretch of forever.

I want your laughter to echo in my nights,
your silence to soothe my storms.

I want the weight of your sorrows,
the light of your joy,
the depth of your being,
woven into the fabric of my existence.

You, my love, are not a passing desire—
you are the eternity my soul longs to hold,
the only forever I will ever need.

What I felt with her,
what I feel for her—
I have never known it before,
and no matter how hard I try,
I cannot feel it for another.

It is as if my heart
was shaped in the mold of her soul,
and now, no one else fits.

Perhaps it is her essence I love,
the eternal breath of her being.

For who else could carry
the scent of my dreams,
the rhythm of my silences?

The world is vast, yet empty,
for there is no one like her.
No one who stirs my spirit
in the way she does.

I searched, but nothing matches
the fire she lit within me.

It is not her face, her touch—
it is her soul

that has become my home.

She is the measure,
the unreachable horizon of my love.
Every attempt to love another
feels like whispering in an empty room—
a sound that fades before it reaches its destination.

I now know,
she was not just someone I loved—
she was the love itself,
and without her,
the world is a shadow of what it once was.

Again and again,
our souls find their way back,
like tides drawn to the moon,
like whispers returning to silence.

Again, we are hurt.
I bleed in longing,
She drowns in the distance.

I have always wanted her near,
but love is not always enough—
not when fate stands in the way.

I reach for her,
She pushes me away.

Her words cut,
her silence burns,
yet my love refuses to fade.

She is cruel, yet I forgive.
She is distant, yet I stay.

Time after time,
I forget the pain
only to fall for her once more—
as if love has no memory,

only devotion.

I deserve to be loved,
not for the pieces I give away,
but for the vast ocean of love
that swells within me.

I am not an empty vessel,
waiting to be filled.
I am the sun, burning bright,
offering warmth without asking.

I carry so much love—
it overflows, it pours,
it seeks not a return,
but simply a heart
willing to hold it.

To love me is not a favor,
it is a meeting of two flames.
I am ready to be seen,
to be cherished,
for all that I am,
And all that I give.

Years passed,
and the tides shifted.
I learned—things would never be the same.
The past was a door
that no longer opened,
and I stopped knocking.

I accepted her,
not as she was,
but as she became.

I accepted the silence,
the distance,
the way she looked at me
but never truly saw me anymore.

I never wanted to lose her,
so I whispered,
"Let's be friends."
She smiled and told the world,
"We are good friends."

Yet, we were strangers in disguise.
No calls, no touch,
just a fragile thread of words
that surfaced once in a while.

Still, I told myself—
At least she is here.
At least sometimes, we speak.
At least, in some way, she remains.

We spoke—sometimes.
Words, light as feathers,
drifting between us, never too much,
never too deep.

I told myself—
let these feelings rest,
let them wear the mask of friendship.

I never spoke of the past,
never traced the love we once held,
for she wished to keep it untouched,
a memory untainted,
never to be seen in a broken light.

So, like strangers,
we began again,
not from where we left off,
but from a place where nothing was ever said.

A hello, a nod,
small moments stolen from time.
But always, beneath my breath,
a quiet fear remained—
"What if she leaves again?"

No matter how heavy my heart,
I never let her see the storm.
I wore my happiness like armor,
smiling, even when it hurt.

She never called, never asked,
never sent a message my way.
Yet, one night,
I whispered my longing into the world—
"I miss you."

And she answered.
"I love you."

At that moment,
the ache melted into light.
I poured my heart into words,
told her again and again—
"I have loved you, I will always love you."

She spoke softly,
*"Even if we never meet again,
even if we don't talk,
I will carry you in my prayers."*

Love does not always stay in touch,
but it never truly leaves.

For a moment, she pulls me close,
her words warm like the sun.

And just when I start to believe,
she pushes me away,
like waves retreating from the shore.

One day, I am hers—
the next, I am nothing.
I do not understand her tides,
her shifting skies.
She loves, she leaves,
she returns, only to go again.

But still, my heart waits,
captive to the rhythm of her moods,
aching for the days when she stays.

I have loved her,
I love her still,
and I will love her for as long
as my heart remembers its beat.

But love should not be
a wound I keep reopening,
a cycle of warmth and cold,
of holding on and being pushed away.

I am tired.
Not of love,
but of this endless waiting,
of hoping for something that never stays.

So, I will not run from my feelings,
nor will I chase her shadows.
I accept what is,
and I free myself from what is not.

Love will remain,
but I will not beg it to stay.
My life is mine to live—
fully, freely, without fear.

It is not words that bind,
my love,
but the silent vows of the soul.

You speak of presence,
yet your steps vanish
before my longing arms
can hold them.

I do not rage,
nor do I curse the wind—
I only ache with the knowing
that love,
when spoken but not lived,
wounds deeper than silence ever could.

You whisper of forever,
yet your leaving is
etched in the quiet,
in the spaces where I reached
and found only the echo of my yearning.

Do you not see?
I do not need a moment of you,
I need the weight of your being—
the stillness of love that does not drift
with the restless tide of time.

But you go, my darling,
like the sun slipping beneath the sea,
leaving only a trace of gold upon the waves—
a promise I hold
even as the night swallows it whole.

I step lightly around you,
afraid that my words
might stir your storms.
Yet, do you not see how your silence
cuts me deeper than a thousand swords?
How your careless words
leave scars upon the fragile
corners of my heart?

I know the tempests you cradle within,
the battles unseen behind your gaze.
And still, I stand before you,
whispering to the empty air,
asking how a soul that has known
the depths of my love
can so easily wound me.

You call me a friend,
but what kind of friendship is this?
Friends do not vanish
when the heart wails in its darkest night.
Friends do not wear indifference
as armor against the ones who love them.

No, I cannot be what you name a friend,
for your friendship is an illusion,
a fleeting shadow that fades

when the light of need shines upon it.

I do not curse you, nor do I turn away,
but my heart aches with the knowing—
you, who are my everything,
treat me as if I am nothing more
then the passing wind—
felt, but never held.

I will love you beyond the death of stars,
beyond the breath of the final wind.

Not as a beggar pleading for alms,
nor as a traveler seeking shelter—
but as the sun gives light,
asking nothing in return.

My love is not a barter,
not a cry for your embrace.
It is the ocean kissing the shore,
whether the shore welcomes it or not.

It is the rose that blooms
even if no eyes linger upon its beauty.
I love because my soul was made for love,
not because you were made to receive it.

Your absence does not steal its fire,
your silence does not unwrite its truth.
This love stands unshaken,
whole, sacred,
belonging to no one, yet filling everything.

It was so easy to lose myself in your love,
like a wandering pilgrim finding solace at a sacred shrine.

But to walk away—ah, it is like leaving behind
the only prayer my soul has ever known.

I have seen your love up close,
felt it like the first rains after a lifetime of drought—
a blessing so deep, it became the ground beneath my feet.

How do I step away
from something that feels like the breath in my lungs.

How do I unhear the silent verses
our hearts sang to each other in the language of the unseen?

Your love was not just given,
it was carved into the marrow of my being.

And now, with each step away,
it is as if I am tearing apart the roots of my own existence.

Sometimes, my heart overflows with love for her,
like a river spilling beyond its banks.

And sometimes, I retreat into silence,
a hermit within the temple of my soul.

Some days, my laughter rises like the dawn,
filling the sky with golden light.

On other days, even the sun
cannot chase away the shadows within me.

This heart is both a tempest and a lull,
a sea that sways between devotion and despair.

Yet even in its restless turning,
there is a quiet knowing—
For in every storm,
in every hush,
in every longing breath—
there is love,
there is life,
there is her.

Yesterday, I wished to unlove you,
to tear your name
from the walls of my heart.

But love is not so easily unwoven—
last night, you returned in a dream,
a place where my will is but a whisper.
I saw us as we once were,
untouched by distance,
unburdened by time.

And there it was again,
the love I buried,
rising like the first light of dawn,
soft, inevitable, all-consuming.

I should run,
but love is not a door I can close.
It lingers in the spaces between breaths,
waits in the hush of the night,
finds its way back—
even in dreams, even in silence.

You are not "someone"…
you are the sunrise I whispered to the night,
the longing I placed in the hands of the stars.

What I once called joy was but a flickering candle—
you gave me the sky, burning with endless light.

Wherever I walk, you are the path beneath my feet.
Whatever I dream, you are the voice in my prayer.

You are not just "mine"—
you are the breath that turns my dust into gold,
the silence that speaks the language of my soul.

Two rivers, one ocean. Two flames, one fire.
No "you," no "me"… only love, eternal and whole.

I want you like the sky wants the sun
like the ocean longs for the moon's pull.

I want you with the depth of a prayer whispered in the
dark,
with the ache of a soul that has found its home.

I want to hold you, not just in my arms,
but in every quiet corner of my being.

I want to cry into your skin,
to kiss you until time forgets itself,
to love you in ways the world has not yet learned to speak.

Only you— you are the storm and the stillness,
the fire and the warmth,
the one who has touched the untouched within me.

No one else could ever stir my heart the way you do.
I want you to kiss me like the universe watches,
like the stars lean in to listen.

I want to wake with you, sleep with you,
breathe in your laughter,
carry your burdens when they grow too heavy.
I want your thoughts tangled with mine,
your heartbeat in rhythm with my longing.

I want you to pull me close and whisper
that all will be well,
that love will hold us together.

Show me all of you—
the light and the shadow, the fierce and the fragile.

I want to wipe your tears with my hands,
write love into your scars,
watch the sun rise and set in your eyes.

I want the nights of endless laughter,
the moments of unbearable quiet,
the kind of love that does not ask for permission,
that does not fear the weight of forever.

Most of all,
I want you to love me
as if no one else in the world matters—
because to me, no one else does.

I cannot stay,
yet I cannot leave.

I cannot speak,
yet silence sets fire to my soul.

We are but two wandering stars,
once sharing the same sky,
now bound by longing
yet never touching.

Tell me, beloved,
what shall I do with this love?
It lingers like the scent of
rain upon parched earth,
like an unsaid prayer
that refuses to fade.

The years have passed,
yet it remains—
not as memory,
nor as longing,
but as a truth deeper than time itself.

I have tried to bury it beneath reason,
to drown it in distance,
but love is a flame

that does not seek permission to burn.
It does not ask to be welcomed,
nor does it heed the passing of days.

Even now, in the hush of night,
it rises within me—
not to call you back,
not to beg for a return,
but simply to be.

A quiet, endless ache,
a love that was never meant to end.

I love the way you hold me—
not just with your arms, but
with the weight of your presence,
as if the universe itself whispers,
You are safe here.

I love the way you see me—
not just the surface,
but the storm and the silence within,
and still, you choose to stay.

I love the way you smile
when I walk into the room
as if my existence alone is enough to bring you joy.
And I love how that joy becomes mine.

I love the way you laugh,
how your happiness spills
over like light breaking through cracks,
how my laughter, tangled with yours,
feels like a secret only the heavens understand.

I love the way you listen,
as if every word I say is worth hearing,
as if time bends when we speak,
as if even silence between us is a conversation.

I love how you hold my hand,
absent mindedly,
as if to remind me—
I am here, I am with you.

How your presence makes the world quieter,
turning chaos into calm,
fear into trust, distance into home.

I love how I can be myself with you,
in all my randomness,
in all my contradictions.
And how you meet me there—
not to fix, not to change,
but simply to *be.*

I love that nothing about us is perfect,
yet everything feels as if
it was always meant to be.

I love that I am yours,
that you are mine,
that whatever we are—

whoever we become—
in this moment, we just *are.*

I do not know if these words will reach you,
but if they do,
let them rest in your heart,
for they have always been true,
and they always will be.

I love you because,
with you, I am unchained.
No masks, no pretenses—
just the quiet truth of who I am,
laid bare in your presence, without fear.

I love you because even in stillness,
you are there.
Even in silence, you speak.
Even in distance, you remain.

I am not perfect,
yet you do not ask me to be.
You embrace my flaws as if they were sacred.

And I, in turn, love yours—
not as cracks to be mended,
but as verses in a poem only my heart understands.

You, my love, are the quiet knowing,
the unwavering presence,

the sacred echo of a love that existed
long before we ever met.

Does the wind ever whisper my name to you,
the way it carries yours to me?

Do you feel the emptiness where my presence used to be?
Do you ever pause,
lost in a moment you do not understand,
only to realize—it is me,
somewhere in the distance,
longing for you?

Or is it only my heart that still waits,
still aches,
still calls for you in the silence
where your voice once live?

Why does your silence stretch like an endless night,
where even the stars refuse to speak?

Why do the words I ache for
never find their way to me?

Do you not feel the weight of my waiting,
the quiet ache of an unanswered heart?

Or have you woven yourself in forgetfulness,
while my soul still sings your name in the wind?

I try to walk forward,

but your essence clings to me like

the scent of rain on thirsty earth.

I am not just missing you—

I am carrying you,

in every breath, in every silence,

in the spaces you once filled.

Tell me, beloved,

did you leave,

or did you plant yourself so deeply within me

that I can no longer tell where you end and I begin?

I have seen faces glow like the first light of dawn,
heard voices drift like songs from another life.

I have met souls as soft as autumn winds,
but none of them carried her shadow.

I looked for her in fleeting smiles,
in the warmth of unfamiliar hands,
in echoes of a love I tried to replace—
but she was not there.

She was never just a name, never just a memory.
She was the silence between my heartbeats,
the ache that lingers when all else fades.

Others arrived, others remained,
but love is not a wandering traveler.
It does not change its home,
does not call another by her name.
Mine, my love, was spoken into existence for her.

Her place remains, untouched by time,
a quiet ache, a name whispered in the wind.

If not her, then no one—
for love does not mold itself to new hands,
it does not wear another's face.

Where could I find another like her?
The moon does not ask for a second sun,
the ocean does not search for a different shore.

She was, she is, she will always be—
a space within me
that no one else can ever fill.

Just once, I want to hear her say it—
not in whispers lost to the wind,
not in the silence that stretches between us,
but with trembling lips and a heart laid bare.

That she loves me, as fiercely as I love her.
That this distance is not her desire,
but a weight she carries, just as I do.
That every night, she turns in longing,
every morning, she wakes with my name still resting on her
lips.

Does she, too, pause before reaching out?
Does she type my name only to erase it?
Does she hold back her voice,
even when it aches to call for me?

I know she feels it—
this love, this ache, this pull that refuses to fade.
But she walks away, bound by something unseen,
torn between love and what must be.

If only, just once,
she would let love win.
If only she would stand before me,
eyes full of all she never said,
and whisper—

"Yes, I love you. Yes, I miss you. Yes, it is just as hard for me."

I do not know why she never turned back,
why my longing was not enough to call her home.

I whispered, again and again,
"I need you, I need you,"
but the wind carried my words away,
and she never heard them land at her feet.

Was my ache too quiet?
Or was her heart too far to feel it?

I do not know.
I only know that I called,
and she kept walking.

She is not mine, nor will she ever be.
Our paths are rivers that will never meet,
our fates like stars in distant skies.

But how does one unlove the soul
that taught them how to feel?
I told myself to move on,
but the road forward felt empty—
there was nothing to walk toward.

She raised the skies of my longing so high
that the ground beneath feels unworthy.
How do I settle for shadows
when I have tasted the sun?

I carry her absence as if it were presence,
her memory like an eternal echo.
I do not choose this love—
this love decides me.

In the silence where the world fades,
she comes—
not as a shadow, not as a memory,
but as something weightless,
like air moving through my ribs,
like a secret only my soul remembers.

Years have turned, yet love does not answer to time.
She does not vanish, does not decay—
she remains, unshaken,
like a light that refuses to dim.

Once, our souls were threads in the same weave,
held together by something neither seen nor named.
But fate is a quiet hand,
pulling us toward roads we never chose.

Another life holds me now,
another name whispers beside mine.
Yet love does not obey the borders of choice.

The heart is an ocean, vast and unending,
and in its quiet depths, she still exists—
not as regret, not as a weight,
but as truth, pure and unbroken.
Though distance stretches wide,
our spirits meet where time dissolves.

I send no plea into the night,
no wish, no demand—
only a knowing, a silent offering,
for love once stood here.

It does not beg, it does not fade.
It simply is—
an ember that never surrenders to ash,
a presence, unseen yet eternal.

Tonight, the air feels heavier,
each breath carrying her name.
I ache for her to appear,
as if the universe might fold
and place her beside me,
like a dream turned flesh.
I long to hold her,
to press my soul against hers
in an embrace that mends the years
we let slip between us.
To speak the words unspoken,
to unravel the silences
woven into the fabric of time.
Let me cry into her arms,
dissolve my sorrow in her warmth,
and find, even for a moment,
the peace I have forgotten.

Oh, if only she would call,
her voice would quench this fire,
her question, "How are you?"
would rebuild a world
where I am whole once more.

You were not just someone I loved,
you became the gravity that held my world together,
the unseen thread weaving through my existence.

You turned into the story my hands wouldn't close,
the dream my soul refused to wake from.
So I wrote—
not in ink, but in longing,
filling pages with words too sacred to be spoken,
with feelings too vast to be contained.

I remember the first time my eyes met yours—
as if the universe had been holding its breath,
waiting for that single moment to unfold.

I remember the first words between us,
how they stayed with me long after,
turning my nights into restless echoes,
making me search for you
in the quiet spaces where the world stood still.

I remember the laughter that felt like home,
tears that carried only your name,
secrets passed like whispered prayers,
and silences heavy with the weight of unspoken truths.

I remember your eyes—
not as moons, but as something deeper,
pulling tides within me I did not know existed.

I remember your smile—
not as a sun, but as warmth that reached
the coldest corners of me.

I remember your voice—
not as a melody, but as something my soul
still recognizes in the hush of the wind.

I remember standing close enough to feel you,
yet far enough to know I was losing you.

I remember calling for you in thoughts I never spoke,
only to wake up each day trying to forget.

I remember the joy of finding you—
and the sorrow of knowing
I was never meant to keep you.

In the depth of your gaze, my heart races,

Every glance, a whisper of the divine.

Your eyes, a universe where I lose myself,

I long to stay, forever intertwined.

To leave you is to part with the stars,

For in your gaze, I find my home, soul, and love.

Her words say love,
but her tone stings like thorns.
She speaks to me harshly,
yet promises she will always stay.

How can love be both a balm
and a wound?
How can she hold me close,
then let go so easily?

She once wrote me a letter,
words carved from the
deepest corners of her soul.
Again and again,
she whispered the same truth—
her love was never a cage,
never a chain.

She did not need me by her side to love me.
She only wished for my joy,
no matter where I stood,
no matter whose hand I held.

She could bear the distance,
the silence,
even the weight of a life without me—
but my sorrow,
that was the one thing
she could never endure.

Her love asked for nothing,
but gave me everything.

Loving you was as simple as the dawn—
it arrived without effort, filling everything.

But forgetting you?
That is a burden no heart should bear.
It is asking fire to forget how to burn,
or the sky to abandon its endless blue.

To unlove you would be to erase
the very threads of my soul.
Even in your absence,
you live in every corner of me,
a love that refuses to be undone.

She never let go of my hand.
Through the hush of the moon,
through the chaos of nameless streets,
even in the sorrow of parting—
her fingers sought mine,
as if drawn by a truth older than time.

She did not hold me out of habit,
but as if the stars had whispered
that our hands must never part.
And when words failed,
she would lift my hand to her lips,
pressing a kiss like a sacred prayer,
as if whispering, *You are known. You are safe.*

It was never just a touch.
It was the soul speaking without sound,
a vow deeper than ink could write.
A warmth unchained by time,
unshaken by distance,
woven into eternity.

I search my heart for anger,
for a reason to turn away,
but love whispers—
there is none.

How can I hate you,
when all I hold are the echoes
of your laughter,
the warmth of your words,
the softness of memories
that refuse to fade?

I tell myself to move on,
to walk a path where you do not exist,
but love is not a door one can shut.
It lingers like a fragrance,
woven into the air I breathe.

If forgetting means to hate,
then I will never forget.
For in my heart,
there is only love,
and love knows no hate.

She poured tenderness into my fractures,
her love a balm, her presence a refuge.
And even now,
as she wraps herself in cruelty like borrowed armor,
as her words cut sharp as winter's wind,
I still see the hands that once held me gently,
the soul that once sheltered mine.
Even if she turns into a storm,
I will stand beneath her rain,
for I cannot unlove
the one who once made me whole.

If we are not meant to walk this path together,

if the tides of life pull us apart,

know this—love does not vanish with distance.

Even in separation, I remain,

rooted in the love I carry for you.

It is not a fleeting fire,

but an eternal glow that neither time nor fate can dim.

I wish I could hold you forever,
but if not, let me hold you in the quiet chambers of my
heart,
where your laughter still echoes,
where the dreams we wove together still bloom.

You have shown me love in its purest form—
unshaken, unafraid, untouched by the weight of the world.
I will carry it with me always,
a light in the dark, a prayer on my lips.

And if not in this lifetime,
then in another,
where our souls will meet again,
like rivers returning to the sea.

My world rises with you like the sun,
and sets in the shadow of your absence.

Every path I walk leads back to you,
every breath I take carries your name.

I have searched for an escape,
but love is a circle—
wherever I go, I find you waiting.

Even if I am just a name
you once whispered,
even if I am only a shadow in your past,
know this—
I still carry your dreams in my heart.

I want to see you rise,
to touch every star
you once pointed at,
to walk every path you
spoke of with fire in your eyes.

Even if my footsteps no longer
walk beside yours,
I pray the wind carries you forward.

Love does not wither with distance,
it does not demand to be seen.
It simply stands, quietly,
watching from afar,
smiling when you bloom.

And one day, when you stand
where you always wished to be,

know that somewhere, in some silent prayer,
I am still rooting for you.

I could never hate you—

for love does not turn to dust,

it does not sour with distance.

It only changes form,

becoming a silent prayer,

a blessing whispered into the wind.

Be happy, be whole,

and let laughter bloom in your days.

May kindness embrace you,

and may love find you in every corner of your life.

Even from afar, I smile when you shine.

Even in silence, I send you my prayers.

Like a whisper,
you slipped into my thoughts,
soft as a breeze, inevitable as the tide.

I did not call for you, yet you arrived—
filling the spaces I never knew were empty,
turning absence into longing, longing into love.

Now, you are everywhere.
In the hush of dawn, in the hush of my heart,
in the pages I turn and the dreams I cradle.

No matter how far the world may place you,
you remain—
not just in my thoughts,
but in the essence of who I am.

Suddenly, every page holds your breath,
every word aches with your presence.

My hands move, but it is my heart that writes—
etching you into verses,
trapping you between ink and silence.

I do not know how to stop.
How does one silence love
when it flows like a river,
when it rises like the moon,
when it burns like the sun?

Even if I put down my pen,
you will remain—
between the spaces,
in the unwritten lines,
in the quiet longing of every pause.

The seasons have folded over us,
years unraveling like
a thread from an old tapestry,
but time has only learned
to rearrange my longing—
never to erase it.

I do not speak,
but my heart calls your name.
I do not reach,
yet my hands ache for your touch.

Some nights, I wonder if
you still stand by the window,
watching the moon as I do,
our separate worlds stitched together
by the same quiet glow.

I love her,
not as rain longs to meet the earth,
nor as a river aches for the sea,
but as the sun adores the distant moon—
watching, illuminating, never needing to hold.

She moves like a river untamed,
while I am the wind,
whispering to her as she flows.

I do not ask her to stay,
for she is already everywhere—
in the breath between my words,
in the hush of my longing.

I love her in the quiet language of stars,
where no touch is needed,
where silence speaks louder than sound.

She lingers in the spaces between my thoughts,
like an echo that never fades,
like a dream that never wakes.

She is here, even when she is not.

Her absence is not a void,

but a presence unseen.

She walks alone,
strong as the winds that shape the mountains,
her soul vast as the open sea.

Her smile warms the coldest shadows,
her kindness is a treasure
the world can barely hold.

She carries her battles in silence,
yet the storms bow to her strength.
In her, I see a light
that turns darkness into dawn.

She is my anchor, my flame,
the song my soul sings in its quiet moments.
Her joy is my prayer,
her freedom, my greatest wish.

Every note in a song carried your name,
and every pause in music felt like the space you left behind.
Time itself seemed to slow
as if the world refused to turn without you.

I have kept everything—
the rose she placed in my hands,
its petals still holding the whisper of her touch.

The letters she wrote, ink trembling,
as if her heart bled between the lines.

I have kept her laughter tucked away,
the way it spilled into the quiet,
filling spaces I never knew were empty.

Her voice, a secret melody,
still lingers in the hush of night.

Her smile is folded into my soul,
pressed between memories like a fragile petal.

Each stolen glance, each unspoken word—
they live in the chambers of my heart,
untouched by time.
Even the ache, I have not let go—
her silences, her storms,
the way she made me laugh
just to keep me from shattering.

What can I say?
I remember everything.

I have kept it all.

Where do I find the peace
you once placed in my hands?
Where do I search for the love
that flowed from your soul into mine?
You came like the moon in my night,
soft, luminous, eternal—
only to vanish,
leaving me lost in the dark you left behind.
You were the only prayer ever answered,
the only song that felt like home.

Forgetting you is not in my power,
and loving you less is beyond my will.

Each day, love rises within me,
relentless as the sun,
burning, growing, consuming.

What have I become, beloved?
A wanderer in the desert of your absence,
etching my longing into the wind,
hoping it carries my heart
back to you.

O Universe,
I ask for nothing but a single day—
A day where time bends,
where moments stretch into lifetimes.
Let me gather my whole existence
into those fleeting hours,
Let me love in a way that eternity can hold.

Let me see her laughter one more time,
the way it spills like light into the shadows of my heart.
Let me listen to her voice,
the melody that still lingers
in the silence of my nights.

Let me look into her eyes,
and find the love that once made my soul believe.

Let me whisper my sorrow,
lay my regrets at her feet,
ask for forgiveness where words once failed.

Let me hold her,
feel the peace that only she can bring,
a stillness that even the universe cannot replace.

Let me love her—
not just for that day,

but with a love so full, so boundless,
that it stays with her for all the days to come.

And when the night wraps
us in its quiet embrace,
let me rest my head against her chest,
feel her arms around me as if they were home,
and as sleep takes me,
let her press a kiss upon my forehead—
a farewell, a blessing, a promise
that in some way, somewhere,
we will meet again.

I send these words with no chains, no plea.
Love does not hold, it does not press—
it only stands, unwavering.

I do not stir the past,
I only let my heart speak its truth—
that you are still the light within me,
a glow that does not bend to time.

Wherever this road may take us,
know this—
you are not lost to me.

You are written into the marrow of my soul,
a love that does not disappear,
but changes shape,
like the sea meeting the shore,
again and again, forever.

I hope her heart is at ease,
that her days are touched by gentle winds.

I wish the weight she carries feels lighter,
and the battles she fights grow softer.

Even in her silence, I send my prayers,
whispering to the universe to hold her gently.

May she be safe, may she find joy,
and may her soul always know its strength.

I tried, again and again,

to hold her within the walls of my life,

but like the wind, she slipped through my fingers,

moving further each time I reached for her.

I walked towards her,

calling her back to the place we once stood,

but with every step I took,

she drifted farther,

as if the distance between us was meant to grow.

Now, I see—

not all love is meant to be held,

not all stories are meant to last.

I cannot weave a fate

that was never ours, to begin with.

So, I open my hands.

I let go—not in anger, not in sorrow,

but in surrender,

for what is forced is not love,

and what is real will never need to be held too tightly.

This is how it must be,

for both of us.
And I am ready to accept it.

I poured myself into love—
stitched my heart into every moment,
offered every apology my soul could carry,
held you in the gentlest way I knew how.

I tried to mend what was breaking,
tried to keep the light from fading,
but love is not kept by effort alone.
I gave you joy,
but it was never enough to make you stay.

Now, what is left for me to do?
When you no longer ask, no longer want,
when my presence is met with silence—
what do I hold onto?

This ache is heavy,
this emptiness vast.
Yet, I know—one day, I will move forward,
one day, my feet will carry me far from here.

And still, the thought unsettles me—
to walk ahead without you,
to leave behind what once was my world.

For you were not just love,
you were every joy I ever dreamed of.

And if I move beyond you,
what remains for me to find?

I do not seek your apology,
for words cannot mend what the soul has endured.

But one day,
when the weight of silence finds you,
when the wind carries my absence to your heart,
I hope you pause—
and feel what I felt.

Not for my sake,
but so you may understand
what love once stood before you,
and how, with your own hands,
you let it slip away.

I have loved you,
not as one loves another,
but as the sky loves the sun—
without need, without end, without fear.

Loving you was loving the echo of my soul,
a light too sacred to be hidden,
too vast to be caged within silence.

Yet love, my dear, is not meant to linger
at a door that never opens,
nor to be poured into hands
that let it slip like passing rain.

I have given you the rivers of my heart,
but you held them like water—
never knowing the
weight of the ocean you carried.

And so, I sit with the truth,
not in sorrow, nor regret,
but in the quiet knowing
that I was never meant to shrink to be loved.

For years, I buried my longing,
and hid it beneath the sands of time.
But why should love be silenced,

when it is the holiest
prayer my soul has ever known?

Loving you was never a sin—
it was the closest I have come to the divine.

But you, my love,
are seeking another dawn,
a flame that is not mine to keep.

And so, I release you—not in anger,
but in the wisdom of my worth.

This love, it does not fade;
it lingers, written in the deepest corners of my soul,
not bound by time, nor by longing,
but by the beauty of love itself.

I do not leave empty—
I leave whole.
For love was never
about being claimed,
but about knowing when to set a caged bird free.

And though I let you go,
this love will breathe
within me until my last breath—

not as a wound,

but as the most sacred gift I ever gave myself.

Let's end here—
not with anger, not with sorrow,
but with the quiet acceptance
that some love is not meant to be held,
only remembered.

Go on, find your peace.
Let your heart be light,
let your days be free of longing.
I will not call you back,
nor will I beg time to turn.

And yet—
when the world quiets,
when the night hums with loneliness,
I will write.

For the writing of you became my refuge,
my way of keeping you close,
without ever asking you to stay.

So go, if you must.
But in ink, in verses, in the spaces between words—
you will always remain.

Some stories remain unfinished,
not because love was not strong enough,
but because fate had other plans.

Yet my love does not crumble with distance,
it does not fade with time.
It lingers, like an unspoken prayer,
like a flame burning in the unseen corners of my soul.

I bow before destiny, knowing it has won,
but not without sorrow, not without longing.
Still, somewhere beyond this moment,
in another lifetime, in a world yet unwritten,
I will find you again.

And maybe then, in that place beyond time,
you will finally know—
how deeply, how truly,
I have always loved you.

When no voice calls your name at dawn,

when no footsteps linger in the hush of night,

when the world stretches before you, boundless and vast—

is this the breath of freedom,

or the sigh of loneliness?

Is it the soul unchained,

dancing where no eyes follow,

where no hands pull, no hearts demand?

Or is it the heart untethered,

adrift in an ocean with no shore,

calling out to the wind,

only to hear its echo return?

To walk alone is to taste the sky,

to hold the sun in your palms,

to move like the river,

answering to no one but the tide.

But what is flight,

if no one waits for your wings to return?

Tell me, love—

is solitude a blessing,

or a wound that does not bleed?

Is silence a gift,

or the absence of what once made you whole?

Last night, I met you in a dream,
as if time had bent in mercy,
as if the stars conspired to let us touch
what the world had kept apart.

Your eyes met mine—
a sunrise after endless dusk,
a warmth I had forgotten how to hold.

We moved toward each other,
not in the wild embrace of longing,
but in the quiet ache of restraint.

No arms wrapped around me,
only fingers grazing in a fleeting handshake—
a love too vast for touch,
too wounded for claiming.

Yet my heart, this reckless wanderer,
raced as it always did in your presence,
a bird that never learned that
the sky was no longer home.

You stood apart
as if tethered to a world that had no place for me.
Still, I drew near, my soul reached.

But you— you stood unmoved,
not refusing, not inviting,
a silent doorway to what once was.

Then the world grew quiet— just you and I,
breathing the same air,
lost on a balcony
where time held its breath.

I wrapped my arms around you from behind,
not to claim,
not to plead,
but simply because my being knew no
other way to exist near you.

You did not pull away, nor did you lean in—
a love allowed to burn,
but never to be named.

And then you asked,
as if the wind carried your voice
from some distant life—
"What do you want?"

Ah, my love, how could you not know?
With the weight of a thousand lifetimes,

with the certainty of the sun and moon,

I whispered the only truth I have ever known—
"You. For a lifetime."